The Beginner's Guide to a Plant-based Diet

Easy Beginner's Cookbook with Plant-Based Recipes for Healthy Eating & a 3-Week Plant-Based Diet Meal Plan to Reset & Energize Your Body

Table of contents:

Chapter 6. Desserts & Snacks...................... 104

Chapter 7. Homemade Basics, Sauces, and Condiments 124

Introduction

Broadly speaking, a human diet is categorized into two parts, plant-based and the animal-based foods. When comparing nutritional values, the plant-sourced foods offer more than animal-based food. From macronutrients including carbohydrates, proteins, and fats to the vitamins and minerals which are essential to the human body, everything can be sourced from plants making animal protein less important in a healthy, well-balanced diet.

While this wasn't widely accepted for some time, scientific discoveries and years of research on the human diet, has brought forth the trust and confidence that people developed in plant-based diets. This it is mainly because of the health benefits such food provides. Consuming an all plant-based diet can prevent a person from eating health-damaging saturated fats and other harmful elements that could lead to toxicity in the body or increase one's risk for certain illnesses.

While discussing the merits of this diet and the dos and don'ts of it, you'll also learn the basics of the diet and find useful recipes that fit into this specific diet plan. All recipes are divided into broad categories suitable to meet your daily needs, from breakfast to entrees, snacks, desserts, condiments, and more.

What is a Plant-based Diet?

Vegan, vegetarian, or plant-based? With so much dietary jargon everywhere, it is difficult to distinguish between them. To put it simply, a plant-based diet is anything sourced from plants whether it's vegetables, fruits, grains, oils, milk, seeds, nuts, flours, or legumes. This diet restricts the consumption of animal-based food items whether it's animal meat, milk/dairy or fats. Due to these features, we can say that a plant-based diet is another term for a vegan diet as both the diets are highly restrictive on animal consumption, even if it's eggs or processed dairy. Every ingredient should be sourced from plants. In this sense, a vegetarian diet is a slightly different approach since it doesn't restrict the use of eggs, yogurt, cheese, etc. In a plant-based diet, these should be replaced with vegan substitutes.

Benefits of a Plant-based Diet

A plant-based diet has proven health effects due to the composition of the foods. Reduced consumption of saturated fats prevents various diseases, including cardiovascular problems, high cholesterol levels, and obesity. The following are other guaranteed benefits of this diet:

Weight and BMI Control

Research studies conducted on the plant-based diet have revealed that people who follow it tend to have lower BMI or body mass index, reduced risk of obesity, and a lower chance of heart disease and diabetes. This is mainly because plant-based diets deliver more fibers, water, and carbohydrates in the body. This may keep the body's metabolism up and running properly while providing a good boost of continuous energy.

Back in 2018, a study was conducted on this diet plan and it was found to be the most effective for treating obesity. In that study, 75 people with obesity or weight problems were given a completely vegan plant-based diet and their results were compared with those consuming animal-based diets. After four months of this experiment, the plant-based diet group showed a significant decrease in their body weight (as much as 6.5 kilograms). They all effectively lost more the fat mass and showed an improvement in insulin sensitivity. Another study involving 60,000 individuals showed similar results with people on a vegan diet recording the lowest body mass index compared to vegetarians and animal-based dieters.

Lower risk of heart disease and other conditions

The American Heart Association recently conducted a study in which middle-aged adults who were on a plant-based diet were studied. All the subjects showed a decrease in their rate of heart disease. Based on the results of this research, the association has listed the following diseases which can be prevented through a plant-based diet:

- Heart stroke
- High blood pressure
- High cholesterol levels
- Certain cancers
- Type II diabetes
- Obesity
- Diabetes

Plant-based diets also help manage diabetes as it improves insulin sensitivity and fights against insulin resistance. Out of all the 60,000 participants in the study, about 2.9 percent on the vegan diet had Type II diabetes, while 7.6 percent of participants following nonvegetarian diets presented with type II diabetes. From this observation, the researchers confirmed that a plant-based diet could help in the treatment of diabetes. It was also proposed that this diet can help diabetic patients lose weight, improve metabolic rates and decrease their need for medical treatments.

It was also suggested that doctors should recommend this diet as part of the treatment for people with type II diabetes or prediabetes. While medical treatments ensure short term results, the plant-based dietary approach offers long term results.

What to Eat and What to Avoid?

There is a long list of foods allowed on the plant-based diet including grains, fruits, vegetables, legumes, seeds, oils, and nuts. Here are detailed lists of some foods you can freely consume on the plant-based diet.

Fruits

Since all fruits come from plants, they're all safe to eat while following a plant-based diet. This is different than other popular diets that disallow most fruits due to their sugar content. Some fruits you can enjoy are:

- Apples
- Citrus fruits
- Berries
- Bananas
- Grapes
- Melons
- Avocado

Vegetables

Where other diets are restrictive on the types of veggies allowed, the plant-based diet includes all vegetables without any limitations. However, fiber-rich veggies are preferable especially leafy greens which are rich sources of minerals and vitamins. Some vegetables you can safely eat on a plant-based diet are:

- Cauliflower
- Broccoli
- Kale
- Beetroot
- Asparagus
- Carrots
- Tomatoes
- Peppers
- Zucchini

There are other vegetables rich in carbohydrates and vitamins. These are allowed on this diet, too. They include most root vegetables including:

- Potatoes
- Beets
- Sweet potato
- Butternut squash

Legumes

Legumes are a basic and vital part of the plant-based diet. They greatly compliment the other plant-based ingredients as they are rich in both carbs and protein along with vitamins. Legumes are basically the underground part of a plant used to store most of its nutrients which is why they're so beneficial. Examples of these are:

- Black beans
- Chickpeas
- Lentils
- Peas
- Kidney beans

Seeds

Seeds, even when consumed in a very small amount, provide a lot of vitamins and minerals. For example, sesame seeds contain a significant amount of vitamin E. Other seeds allowed in the plant-based diet are:

- Pumpkin seeds
- Chia seeds
- Hemp seeds
- Flax seeds

Nuts

Like seeds, you will also find nuts to be an essential source of all vitamins, healthy fats, and antioxidants. Here is a list of nuts allowed on the plant-based diet:

- Almonds

- Pecans
- Brazil nuts
- Cashews
- Macadamia nuts
- Pistachios

Healthy fats

The best part about the plant-based diet is the healthy unsaturated fats allowed. They protect the body from bad cholesterol and heart diseases that come along with it. The plant-based oils are allowed:

- Avocado oil
- Walnut oil
- Chia seed oil
- Hemp seed oil
- Flaxseed oil
- Olive oil
- Canola oil

Whole grains

Another source of carbohydrates whole grains are also rich in minerals and fiber. They can help maintain blood sugar levels and form a vital part of this healthy diet. Here are all the whole grains used in this diet:

- Brown rice
- Oats
- Spelt
- Buckwheat
- Quinoa
- Wholegrain breads
- Rye
- Barley

The products obtained or extracted from those whole grains are also usable on this diet, including flours, whole meals, etc.

Plant-based milk

Since animal milk is not allowed on the plant-based diet, there are other plant-sourced options you can eat including:

- Soy milk
- Rice milk
- Almond milk
- Coconut milk
- Oat milk
- Hemp milk
- Almond milk

All these milks have their own distinct taste and texture and should be used accordingly. Look for unsweetened varieties for all-purpose use.

Foods to Avoid

Well, it has been established that all animal-based foods are not allowed on the plant-based diet, but there are other products not allowed on a plant-based diet. Here is a detailed list:

- Animal meat ranging from poultry, seafood, pork, lamb, and beef
- Butter, ghee, and other solid animal fats
- All processed foods
- Sugary foods items such as cookies, cakes, and pastries
- All refined white carbohydrates
- Processed vegan and vegetarian alternatives which may contain added salt or sugar
- Excessive salt
- Deep-fried food

Eight Food-Based Mistakes

Without a clear understanding of the diet, people may commit certain mistakes while following a plant-based diet. This is mainly because of the thin differences between ingredients. The following are common food-based mistakes people usually make and the different ways to avoid them:

- **Bread**

There are countless varieties of bread available today. While all loaves primarily made from a basic flour batter, there are many additional ingredients which may compromise the plant-based diet. Adding butter, animal milk, fats or other animal products or excessive sugar and salt may make bread unsuitable for a plant-based diet. Make sure to check the ingredients of the store-bought breads thoroughly or prepare bread at home using only vegan ingredients.

- **Soup Stock**

Stocks and broths are commonly used in soups and curries but most are liquid extracts of bones, meat, and vegetables. Since chicken and beef stocks are usually used in popular soup recipes, people use them even on a plant-based diet. Vegetable stocks and broths should be used instead. Stock gets most of its nutrients and fats from the meat or bones they are cooked in, this is why only vegetable stocks are recommended for this diet.

- **Pasta**

Whole wheat pasta or basic flour pasta is a great option to enjoy some flavors and variety on the plant-based diet. Adding pasta to your plant-based menu is not harmful at all, but if the same pasta is cooked with animal-sourced ingredients it is unsuitable for this diet. Vegetable pasta recipes, including zucchini noodles, are also a great option for this diet.

- **Orange Juice**

Freshly squeezed organic orange juice is not bad for the plant-based diet. In fact, it is a good source of vitamin C. However, when the juice is processed to add extra nutrients, the problem starts. Some companies add vitamin D2 or D3 to the juice. While vitamin D2 is sourced from plants, vitamin D3 is an animal-sourced vitamin which is not allowed on a plant-based diet. Read the labels and do your research to avoid such products. It is better to rely on homemade, freshly squeezed juices instead of store-bought juices.

- **Granola**

Granola comes in a wide variety. Due to the diversity of the ingredients used in different granola recipes, a person on a plant-based should be more careful in their selection. Granola may contain dairy like milk, butter, or eggs. Those should be completely avoided. Instead, choose one made of oats, nuts, seeds, and plant fats while on this diet.

- **Creams and Creamers**

Since all creams or cream cheese are obtained from animal milk, they are disallowed on a plant-based diet even in small amounts. Instead, plant-based nondairy creamers should be used. Creamers obtained from soy or coconut milk have a good taste and a rich thick texture just like other creams.

- **Cheese**

Cheese is a staple in most diets but are animal-based and now allowed, as previously stated. That's where vegan cheese kick in. These cheeses are prepared from plant-based ingredients including soy, nuts, tapioca, coconut, root vegetables, or aquafaba. Like dairy cheese, vegan cheese varies in forms, texture, and taste but they do provide a good substitute for animal-based cheese.

- **Veggie Sausages & Burgers**

Burgers and sausages are commonly enjoyed and hard to say no to. Fortunately, now both burgers and sausages come in plant-based varieties. These burgers and sausages look more like the meat-based sausages and burgers but are made out of shredded vegetables and a batter. Always opt for these varieties while following a plant-based diet.

Chapter 1. The Plant-Based 21-day Meal Plan

Week 01

Day 1:

Breakfast: Golden Milk Smoothie
Lunch: Matzo Parsnip Soup
Snack: Baked Sesame Fries
Dinner: Mixed Vegetable Platter
Dessert: Hawaiian Shave Ice

Day 2:

Breakfast: Chickpea Omelet
Lunch: Chickpea Pasta Soup
Snack: Crispy Cauliflower
Dinner: Grilled Chopped Veggies
Dessert: Butterscotch Tart

Day 3:

Breakfast: Zucchini Blueberry Smoothie
Lunch: Cream of Broccoli Soup
Snack: Spinach Mushroom Pockets
Dinner: Garlic Grilled Vegetables
Dessert: 4-Ingredient Brownies

Day 4:

Breakfast: Polenta with Cranberries
Lunch: Sour Cabbage Soup
Snack: Breaded Tofu
Dinner: Marinated BBQ Vegetables
Dessert: Vegan Lemon Cake

Day 5:

Breakfast: Avocado Banana Green Smoothie
Lunch: Sweet Potato Bean Soup
Snack: Raisin Protein Balls
Dinner: Stir-Fry Vegetables
Dessert: Hawaiian Shave Ice

Day 6:

Breakfast: Gingery Mango Smoothie
Lunch: Tomato Rasam Soup
Snack: Cheese Cucumber Bites
Dinner: Chinese Vegetable Stir-Fry
Dessert: Butterscotch Tart

Day 7:

Breakfast: Apple-Lemon Bowl
Lunch: Kale, Lentil, & Beet Salad
Snack: Hibiscus Tea
Dinner: Vegetable Satay
Dessert: 4-Ingredient Brownies

Week 02

Day 1:
Breakfast: Green Spirulina Smoothie
Lunch: Quinoa Kale Salad
Snack: Turmeric Ginger Tea
Dinner: Ginger Vegetable Stir-Fry
Dessert: Vegan Lemon Cake

Day 2:
Breakfast: Ginger Kale Smoothie
Lunch: French-Style Potato Salad
Snack: Moroccan Spiced Eggnog
Dinner: Winter Vegetable Hash
Dessert: Hawaiian Shave Ice

Day 3:
Breakfast: Apple-Lemon Bowl
Lunch: Squash, Pecan, & Pomegranate Salad
Snack: Vanilla Soy Eggnog
Dinner: Matzo Parsnip Soup
Dessert: Butterscotch Tart

Day 4:
Breakfast: Mushroom Scramble
Lunch: Garlic & White Wine Pasta
Snack: Lemon Mint Beverage
Dinner: Chickpea Pasta Soup
Dessert: 4-Ingredient Brownies

Day 5:
Breakfast: Ginger Kale Smoothie
Lunch: Eggplant Vegan Pasta
Snack: Cinnamon Almond Milk
Dinner: Cream of Broccoli Soup
Dessert: Vegan Lemon Cake

Day 6:
Breakfast: Apple-Lemon Bowl
Lunch: Tomato Pesto Pasta
Snack: Mango Lassi
Dinner: Sour Cabbage Soup
Dessert: Hawaiian Shave Ice

Day 7:
Breakfast: Avocado Banana Green Smoothie
Lunch: Alfredo with Peas
Snack: Cardamom Turmeric Tea
Dinner: Sweet Potato Bean Soup
Dessert: Butterscotch Tart

Week 03

Day 1:
Breakfast: Polenta with Cranberries
Lunch: Eggplant Parmesan Pasta
Snack: Indian Spiced Buttermilk
Dinner: Tomato Rasam Soup
Dessert: 4-Ingredient Brownies

Day 2:
Breakfast: Gingery Mango Smoothie
Lunch: Green Chili Mac 'N' Cheese
Snack: Indian Lemonade
Dinner: Kale, Lentil, & Beet Salad
Dessert: Butterscotch Tart

Day 3:
Breakfast: Chickpea Omelet
Lunch: 3-Color Pasta
Snack: Cheese Cucumber Bites
Dinner: Quinoa Kale Salad
Dessert: Hawaiian Shave Ice

Day 4:
Breakfast: Mushroom Scramble
Lunch: Caramelized Onion Mac 'N' Cheese
Snack: Raisin Protein Balls
Dinner: French-Style Potato Salad
Dessert: Vegan Lemon Cake

Day 5:
Breakfast: Green Spirulina Smoothie
Lunch: Cheesy Garlic Pasta with Ciabatta
Snack: Breaded Tofu
Dinner: Squash, Pecan, & Pomegranate Salad
Dessert: 4-Ingredient Brownies

Day 6:
Breakfast: Golden Milk Smoothie
Lunch: Tomato Red Lentil Pasta.
Snack: Spinach Mushroom Pockets
Dinner: Sour Cabbage Soup
Dessert: Butterscotch Tart

Day 7:
Breakfast: Zucchini Blueberry Smoothie
Lunch: Grilled Vegetables
Snack: Crispy Cauliflower
Dinner: Matzo Parsnip Soup
Dessert: Hawaiian Shave Ice

Bonus: Shopping List

Fruits and Vegetables:

- Spinach
- Asparagus
- Parsley
- Garlic
- Onion
- Potatoes
- Sweet Potatoes
- Zucchini
- Mushrooms
- Kale
- Broccoli
- Bell peppers
- Cauliflower
- Eggplants
- Tomatoes
- Ginger
- Parsnip
- Celery
- Peas
- Yellow squash
- Lemon
- Lime
- Cucumber
- Cabbage
- Beets
- Snap Peas
- Strawberries
- Apricots
- Oranges
- Apples
- Bananas
- Mango
- Pineapple
- Pomegranate
- Dried Apricot
- Cranberries
- Blueberries
- Blackberries
- Avocados

Grains and Legumes:

- Chickpeas
- Brown lentils
- White beans
- Kidney beans
- Polenta
- Quinoa

Oils:

- Sesame Oil
- Avocado Oil
- Olive Oil
- Canola Oil

Nuts And Seeds:

- Almonds
- Walnuts
- Peanuts
- Pinenuts
- Cashews
- Pistachios
- Pecans
- Pumpkin Seeds
- Chia seeds
- Sesame seeds
- Flaxseeds

Non Dairy Items:

- Almond Milk
- Coconut Milk
- Soy Milk
- Vegan Cheese
- Coconut yogurt
- Coconut cream

Miscellaneous:

- Flours
- Salt
- Pesto
- Black pepper
- Pasta
- Red pepper flakes
- Tahini
- Chicken seasonings
- Cayenne pepper
- Paprika
- Cumin
- Nutmeg ground
- Cinnamon ground
- Sugar
- Liquid Stevia
- Tomato sauce
- Thyme (fresh and dried)
- Spirulina
- Oregano (fresh and dried)
- Puff pastry
- Protein powder
- Cocoa powder
- Chocolate chips
- Tofu
- Chai spice
- Maple syrup
- Turmeric
- Bread
- Soy sauce
- Vinegar
- White wine
- Balsamic vinegar
- Rosemary (fresh and dried)

Chapter 2. Smoothies and Breakfasts

Golden Milk Smoothie

Preparation time: 10 minutes
Cooking time: 0 minutes
Total time: 10 minutes
Servings: 1

Ingredients:

- 1 cup frozen banana, ripe & sliced
- 1 cup light coconut milk
- 1/2 tsp ground turmeric
- 1 tbsp fresh ginger
- 1 dash ground cinnamon
- 1 dash black pepper; 1 dash ground nutmeg
- 1 dash ground clove and cardamom
- 1/4 cup fresh carrot juice

For Serving

- 1 tbsp hemp seeds

How to prepare:

1. Prepare the smoothie by throwing all the ingredients into a blender jug.
2. Press the pulse button and blend until well incorporated.
3. Serve chilled.

Nutritional Values:

- Calories 155
- Total Fat 13 g
- Saturated Fat 5 g
- Cholesterol 132 mg
- Sodium 297 mg
- Total Carbs 16 g
- Fiber 2 g
- Sugar 1.5 g
- Protein 2 g

Zucchini Blueberry Smoothie

Preparation time: 10 minutes
Cooking time: 0 minutes
Total time: 10 minutes
Servings: 2

Ingredients:

- 1 large ripe frozen banana, peeled & sliced
- 1 cup wild blueberries
- 1 large stem celery
- 2/3 cup zucchini, sliced
- 1 handful greens
- 1 tbsp hemp seeds
- 1/4 tsp ground cinnamon
- 1 cup light coconut milk
- 1/2 tsp maca powder

How to prepare:

1. Prepare the smoothie by throwing all the ingredients into a blender jug.
2. Press the pulse button and blend until well incorporated.
3. Serve chilled.

Nutritional Values:

- Calories 125
- Total Fat 22 g
- Saturated Fat 11 g
- Cholesterol 122 mg
- Sodium 317 mg
- Total Carbs 15 g
- Fiber 2 g
- Sugar 2.1 g
- Protein 0.6 g

Avocado Banana Green Smoothie

Preparation time: 10 minutes
Cooking time: 0 minutes
Total time: 10 minutes
Servings: 2

Ingredients:

- 1 large frozen banana, peeled & sliced
- 1/2 medium ripe avocado
- 1 scoop plain protein powder
- 1 large handful greens
- 3/4 unsweetened almond milk

Optional add-ins

- 1 tbsp seed of choice
- 1/2 tsp maca
- 1/2 cup frozen cucumber

How to prepare:

1. Prepare the smoothie by throwing all the ingredients into a blender jug.
2. Press the pulse button and blend until well incorporated.
3. Serve chilled.

Nutritional Values:

- Calories 131
- Total Fat 13 g
- Saturated Fat 8 g
- Cholesterol 212 mg
- Sodium 321 mg
- Total Carbs 9.7 g
- Fiber 3.1 g
- Sugar 1.8 g
- Protein 2 g

Gingery Mango Smoothie

Preparation time: 10 minutes
Cooking time: 0 minutes
Total time: 10 minutes
Servings: 2

Ingredients:

- 2 1/4 cups frozen mango, chopped
- 1 1/4 cups frozen raspberries
- 1 cup light coconut milk
- 1 medium lime, juiced
- 2 tbsp fresh ginger
- 1 tbsp unsweetened shredded coconut
- 1/8 tsp cayenne pepper
- 1-2 tbsp hemp seeds

For Serving (Optional)

- Coconut Yogurt; Berries
- Shredded coconut; Hemp seeds

How to prepare:

1. Prepare the smoothie by throwing all the ingredients into a blender jug.
2. Press the pulse button and blend until well incorporated.
3. Serve chilled with optional garnishes.

Nutritional Values:

- Calories 141
- Total Fat 9 g
- Saturated Fat 17 g
- Cholesterol 6 mg
- Sodium 23 mg
- Total Carbs 16 g
- Fiber 4 g
- Sugar 3 g
- Protein 3.1 g

Green Spirulina Smoothie

Preparation time: 10 minutes
Cooking time: 0 minutes
Total time: 10 minutes
Servings: 1

Ingredients:

- 1 medium ripe banana
- 1/2 cup cucumber, sliced
- 1 cup light coconut milk
- 1 cup spinach
- 1 tsp spirulina powder
- 1 tbsp hemp seed

For Serving

- 1/4 cup frozen or fresh blueberries
- 1/4 cup granola

How to prepare:

1. Prepare the smoothie by throwing all the ingredients into a blender jug.
2. Press the pulse button and blend until well incorporated.
3. Serve chilled with berries and granola on top.

Nutritional Values:

- Calories 142
- Total Fat 2 g
- Saturated Fat 6 g
- Cholesterol 12 mg
- Sodium 17 mg
- Total Carbs 5 g
- Fiber 3.2 g
- Sugar 10 g
- Protein 1.1 g

Ginger Kale Smoothie

Preparation time: 10 minutes
Cooking time: 0 minutes
Total time: 10 minutes
Servings: 2

Ingredients:

- 1 cup ice
- 2 cups packed kale
- 1 cup ripe frozen mango cubes
- 1 cup ripe frozen peaches
- 1 tbsp minced fresh ginger
- 2 lemons or limes, juiced
- 2 cups of water
- 1 tbsp maple syrup

How to prepare:

1. Prepare the smoothie by throwing all the ingredients into a blender jug.
2. Press the pulse button and blend until well incorporated.
3. Serve chilled.

Nutritional Values:

- Calories 135
- Total Fat 2 g
- Saturated Fat 1 g
- Cholesterol 2 mg
- Sodium 17 mg
- Total Carbs 33 g
- Fiber 1 g
- Sugar 13 g
- Protein 2 g

Mushroom Scramble

Preparation time: 10 minutes
Cooking time: 19 minutes
Total time: 29 minutes
Servings: 6

Ingredients:

- 1 red onion, peeled and diced
- 1 red bell pepper, seeded and diced
- 1 green bell pepper, seeded and diced
- 2 cups mushrooms, sliced
- 1 large head cauliflower, florets
- Sea salt, to taste
- ½ tsp freshly ground black pepper
- 1½ tsp turmeric
- ¼ tsp cayenne pepper
- 3 cloves garlic, peeled and minced
- 2 tbsp soy sauce
- ¼ cup nutritional yeast

How to prepare:

1. First, take a medium skillet and place it over medium heat.
2. Toss in mushrooms and the green and red peppers along with the onion.
3. Stir cook for 8 minutes then add 2 tablespoons water.
4. Toss in cauliflower and continue cooking for 6 minutes.
5. Stir in the turmeric, pepper, salt, cayenne, soy sauce, yeast, and garlic.
6. Cook for another 5 minutes, then serve.

Nutritional Values:

- Calories 284
- Total Fat 7.9 g
- Saturated Fat 1.4 g
- Cholesterol 36 mg
- Sodium 704 mg
- Total Carbs 46 g
- Fiber 3.6 g
- Sugar 5.5 g
- Protein 7.9 g

Apple-Lemon Bowl

Preparation time: 10 minutes
Cooking time: 0 minutes
Total time: 10 minutes
Servings: 2

Ingredients:

- 5 medium apples, any variety
- 6 dates, pitted
- 1 lemon, juiced
- 2 tbsp walnuts
- ¼ tsp ground cinnamon

How to prepare:

1. First, core the apples and dice them into large pieces.
2. Add dates, walnuts, lemon juice, cinnamon, and ¾ apple to a food processor.
3. Blend the apple mixture then top with remaining apples.
4. Serve.

Nutritional Values:

- Calories 134
- Total Fat 4.7 g
- Saturated Fat 0.6 g
- Cholesterol 124mg
- Sodium 1 mg
- Total Carbs 54.1 g
- Fiber 7 g
- Sugar 3.3 g
- Protein 6.2 g

Polenta with Cranberries

Preparation time: 10 minutes
Cooking time: 10 minutes
Total time: 20 minutes
Servings: 4

Ingredients:

- 1/4 cup brown rice syrup
- 2 pears, peeled, cored, and diced
- 1 cup dried cranberries
- 1 tsp ground cinnamon
- 1 cup polenta, cooked

How to prepare:

1. First, heat rice syrup in a saucepan over medium heat.
2. Toss in cranberries, cinnamon, and pears.
3. Mix well and continue cooking for 10 minutes.
4. Divide this mixture over polenta into 4 serving bowls.

Nutritional Values:

- Calories 387
- Total Fat 6 g
- Saturated Fat 9.9 g
- Cholesterol 41 mg
- Sodium 154 mg
- Total Carbs 37.4 g
- Fiber 2.9 g
- Sugar 15.3 g
- Protein 6.6 g

Chickpea Omelet

Preparation time: 10 minutes
Cooking time: 10 minutes
Total time: 20 minutes
Servings: 3 (6-inch) omelets

Ingredients:

- 1 cup chickpea flour
- ½ tsp onion powder
- ½ tsp garlic powder
- ¼ tsp white pepper
- ¼ tsp black pepper
- 1/3 cup nutritional yeast
- ½ tsp baking soda
- 3 green onions, chopped
- 4 oz sautéed mushrooms

How to prepare:

1. Start by whisking chickpea flour with garlic powder, onion powder, black pepper, yeast, baking soda, and white pepper in a large bowl.
2. Stir in 1 cup water while mixing continuously until it forms a smooth batter.
3. Place a nonstick frying pan over medium heat.
4. Pour a dollop of the prepared batter into the pan and cook on low heat.
5. Sprinkle green onions and mushrooms on top.
6. Flip the chickpea omelet and cook for 1 minute.
7. Serve.

Nutritional Values:

- Calories 212
- Total Fat 11.8 g
- Saturated Fat 2.2 g
- Cholesterol 23mg
- Sodium 321 mg
- Total Carbs 14.6 g
- Fibers 4.4 g
- Sugar 8 g
- Protein 7.3 g

Chapter 3. Soup and Salads

Matzo Parsnip Soup

Preparation time: 10 minutes
Cooking time: 72 minutes
Total time: 82 minutes
Servings: 4

Ingredients:

Matzo Balls

- 1 ½ cups quinoa flakes; 1 ½ cups flour
- 2 tsp onion powder; 1 tsp garlic powder
- ¼ tsp sea salt; 2 cups boiling water
- 6 tbsp pumpkin puree

Soup

- 1 medium yellow onion, chopped; ¼ cup coconut aminos
- ½ tsp freshly ground black pepper
- 5 medium carrots, peeled and sliced
- 3 celery stalks, diced; 2 parsnips, peeled and sliced
- 1 cup fresh parsley, chopped; 8 cups vegetable broth

Topping

- 3 tbsp fresh dill, chopped

How to prepare:

1. Start by preheating your over to 300 degrees F.
2. Layer a 15x13-inch baking tray with parchment paper.
3. Prepare the matzo balls by mixing quinoa flakes, onion powder, flour, salt, garlic powder in a mixing bowl.
4. Stir in pumpkin and boiling water, then mix completely.
5. Take a tablespoon of this mixture and roll it into a ball.
6. Make more balls and arrange them on the baking sheet.
7. This will make as many as 30 balls.
8. Bake these balls for 20 minutes in the oven and flip them when cooked halfway through.
9. Allow the matzo balls to cool for 10 minutes.
10. Meanwhile, you can prepare the soup by adding vegetables, black pepper, and coconut aminos to a soup pot.
11. Stir cook for 2 minutes then add the broth.
12. Cook the soup to a boil then reduce the heat to a simmer.
13. Continue cooking for 35 minutes then add matzo balls.
14. Garnish with dill and serve warm.

Nutritional Values:

- Calories 412
- Total Fat 24.8 g
- Saturated Fat 12.4 g
- Cholesterol 3 mg
- Sodium 132 mg
- Total Carbs 43.8 g
- Fibers 3.9 g
- Sugar 2.5 g
- Protein 8.9 g

Chickpea Pasta Soup

Preparation time: 10 minutes
Cooking time: 26 minutes
Total time: 36 minutes
Servings: 6

Ingredients:

- 1 cup onion, diced
- 2 carrots, sliced; 1 celery stalk, diced
- 2 medium potatoes, cubed
- 3 cloves garlic, crushed
- ½ tsp dried thyme
- 4 cups of vegetable broth
- 2 cups of water
- ¼ cup of "chicken" seasoning
- 6 oz cooked pasta
- 2 cups cooked chickpeas
- Salt and pepper, to taste
- Chopped fresh cilantro, to taste

46

Chicken Seasoning

- 1 ⅓ cup of nutritional yeast
- 3 tbsp onion powder
- 1 tbsp garlic powder
- 1 ½ tbsp dried basil
- 1 tsp oregano
- ½ tsp turmeric
- 2 tsp sea salt

How to prepare:

1. Toss onion into a pan and sauté over medium heat for 3 minutes.
2. Stir in celery, potato, and carrots and cook for 3 minutes.
3. Now, mix together chicken seasoning ingredients then add that along with water, broth, thyme, and garlic.
4. Allow the chickpea soup to simmer on medium-low heat for 20 minutes until soft.
5. Toss in cooked pasta and chickpeas.
6. Mix well with pasta and adjust seasoning with salt and black pepper.
7. Garnish with cilantro.
8. Serve.

Nutritional Values:

- Calories 331
- Total Fat 2.5 g
- Saturated Fat 0.5 g
- Cholesterol 35 mg
- Sodium 595 mg
- Total Carbs 69 g
- Fiber 12.2 g
- Sugar 12.5 g
- Protein 8.7g

Cream of Broccoli Soup

Preparation time: 10 minutes
Cooking time: 15 minutes
Total time: 25 minutes
Servings: 6

Ingredients:

- 2 celery stalks, diced
- 1 small carrot, peeled & diced
- ¼ tsp thyme
- 2 big heads f broccoli
- 1 can cannellini beans
- 2 bay leaves
- 4 cups vegetable broth
- 2 cups of water
- 2 tbsp nutritional yeast
- 1 packet Moringa vegetable powder

How to prepare:

1. First, take a large pot and add thyme, celery, and carrot.
2. Cover these veggies and cook for 5 minutes on medium heat.
3. Pour in a splash of water if needed to prevent sticking, then remove them from the heat.
4. Remove the broccoli florets from the stem and chop the stalks after peeling.
5. Now, add the stock, water, bay leaf, beans, and broccoli to the carrot mixture.
6. Cover the soup and cook it to a boil.
7. Then, let the broccoli simmer for 10 minutes approximately.
8. Remove the broccoli soup from the heat and discard the bay leaf.
9. Stir in Moringa and nutritional powder.
10. Blend this soup using an immersion blender until smooth.
11. Garnish as desired.
12. Serve.

Nutritional Values:

- Calories 322
- Total Fat 11.8 g
- Saturated Fat 2.2 g
- Cholesterol 56 mg
- Sodium 321 mg
- Total Carbs 34.6 g
- Fibers 0.4 g
- Sugar 2 g
- Protein 1.1 g

Sour Cabbage Soup

Preparation time: 10 minutes
Cooking time: 62 minutes
Total time: 72 minutes
Servings: 4

Ingredients:

Marination:

- 1 tbsp low-sodium tamari; ¼ tsp liquid smoke
- ½ block firm tofu, drained and diced

Soup:

- 1 cup leek, chopped; 2 tsp garlic, minced
- 6 baby Bella mushrooms, sliced
- 2 tbsp balsamic vinegar
- 3 cups purple cabbage, chopped
- ½ cup bell pepper, chopped
- ½ cup sauerkraut; 1 tsp caraway seeds
- 7 cups vegetable broth; 2 tsp low-sodium tamari
- 1 tbsp Sriracha hot sauce; 1 tbsp lime juice

How to prepare:

1. First, start by preheating the oven to 400 degrees F.
2. Prepare the marinade by mixing liquid smoke and tamari in a bowl.
3. Toss in tofu and mix well until smooth.
4. Allow the tofu to sit for 15 minutes for marination.
5. Spread and set the marinated tofu on a baking tray.
6. Bake the seasoned tofu for 12 minutes approximately at 400 degrees F.
7. Now, place a large soup pot over medium heat.
8. Add leeks with a tablespoon water into this pot and stir cook for 5 minutes.
9. Toss in the garlic and chopped mushrooms.
10. Stir cook for 5 minutes then add vinegar to deglaze the pot.
11. Toss in sauerkraut with its juice, broth, cabbage, bell pepper, hot sauce, caraway seeds, lime juice, and remaining tamari to the soup.
12. Bring this soup to a boil then reduce it to a simmer.
13. Cook for 25 minutes with occasional stirring.
14. Stir in baked tofu and adjust seasoning with salt or other seasonings as needed.
15. Enjoy warm.

Nutritional Values:

- Calories 297
- Total Fat 15.4 g
- Saturated Fat 4.2 g
- Cholesterol 168 mg
- Sodium 203 mg
- Total Carbs 28.5 g
- Sugar 1.1 g
- Fiber 4 g
- Protein 7.9 g

Sweet Potato Bean Soup

Preparation time: 10 minutes
Cooking time: 11 minutes
Total time: 21 minutes
Servings: 4

Ingredients:

- 4, 15-oz cans black beans, drained
- 1 large onion, diced
- 3 garlic cloves, minced
- 2 large carrots, diced
- ½ red bell pepper, diced
- ½ yellow bell pepper, diced
- 2 large sweet potatoes, peeled and diced
- 4 cups vegetable broth
- 2 tsp cumin powder
- 1 tsp coriander powder
- 1 tsp ancho chili powder; ½ tsp salt
- Black pepper, to taste; 3 drops liquid smoke

How to prepare:

1. Start by adding onion and a tablespoon of broth to a pressure cooker.
2. Sauté this onion for 5 minutes approximately on Sauté mode.
3. Stir in minced garlic and stir cook for 1 minute.
4. Toss in rest of the ingredients and then seal the lid.
5. Cook for 5 minutes on Manual mode at High pressure.
6. Once the cooking is done, then release the pressure completely.
7. Remove the cooker's lid and then drain 2 cups of water.
8. Blend with an immersion blender to puree the soup mixture.
9. Serve warm.

Nutritional Values:

- Calories 319
- Total Fat 9.3 g
- Saturated Fat 4.8 g
- Cholesterol 25 mg
- Sodium 101 mg
- Total Carbs 17.8 g
- Sugar 47.9 g
- Fiber 6 g
- Protein 7.2 g

Tomato Rasam Soup

Preparation time: 10 minutes
Cooking time: 1 hr.
Total time: 1 hr. 10 minutes
Servings: 4

Ingredients:

- 1 26-oz container tomatoes, chopped
- 2 cups of water; 1 tsp mustard seeds
- 1 tsp cumin seeds; 1 tsp black pepper
- 1 dried red chili pepper, deseeded
- 5 fresh curry leaves
- 1 tbsp tamarind paste
- 2 tbsp fresh cilantro, chopped
- 1-inch fresh ginger, grated
- 1 tbsp apricot preserves
- 1 tbsp low-sodium soy sauce
- 1 tsp turmeric

How to prepare:

1. Start by throwing all the ingredients into a soup pot.
2. Cover this soup and cook for 1 hour approximately on low heat.
3. Garnish with cilantro.
4. Serve warm.

Nutritional Values:

- Calories 352
- Total Fat 14 g
- Saturated Fat 2 g
- Cholesterol 65 mg
- Sodium 220 mg
- Total Carbs 25.8 g
- Fiber 0.2 g
- Sugar 1 g
- Protein 6 g

Kale, Lentil, & Beet Salad

Preparation time: 10 minutes
Cooking time: 50 minutes
Total time: 60 minutes
Servings: 6

Ingredients:

- 3 medium leeks, chopped
- 1 medium beet, quartered
- 1-2 tbsp olive oil; 1/4 tsp salt
- 1/4 tsp black pepper; 1/2 cup green lentils
- 1 cup vegetable stock
- 4 big handfuls kale, baby spinach, or spring greens

Tahini Dressing

- 1/4 cup tahini; 1/2 medium lemon, juiced
- 2 tbsp maple syrup
- 4 tbsp good olive oil
- 1 pinch each salt and black pepper

How to prepare:

1. Start by preheating the oven to 400 degrees F.
2. Grease a baking tray with cooking spray.
3. Place a saucepan filled with stock and lentils over medium-high heat.
4. Cook for 30 minutes on a simmer then drain.
5. Meanwhile, spread the leeks and beets on a baking tray.
6. Season with salt, black pepper, and olive oil over the veggies.
7. Toss well then bake them for 20 minutes approximately.
8. Meanwhile, prepare the tahini dressing by whisking all of its ingredients in a bowl.
9. Add the beets, leeks, lentils, and greens to a mixing bowl.
10. Toss well then add dressing to the mixture.
11. Stir well and serve.

Nutritional Values:

- Calories 231
- Total Fat 20.1 g
- Saturated Fat 2.4 g
- Cholesterol 110 mg
- Sodium 941 mg
- Total Carbs 20.1 g
- Fiber 0.9 g
- Sugar 1.4 g
- Protein 4.6 g

Quinoa Kale Salad

Preparation time: 10 minutes
Cooking time: 42 minutes
Total time: 52 minutes
Servings: 4

Ingredients:

Quinoa

- ¾ cups quinoa, well rinsed; 1 ½ cups water

Vegetables

- 4 large carrots, chopped; 1 whole beet, thinly sliced
- 2 tbsp water; 1 pinch sea salt
- ½ tsp curry powder

Dressing

- 1/3 cup tahini; 2-3 tbsp lemon juice
- 1-2 tbsp maple syrup
- 1 pinch sea salt; 1/4 cup water

Salad

- 8 cups kale, chopped

- ½ cup cherry tomatoes, chopped
- 1 ripe avocado, cubed
- ¼ cup hemp seeds
- ½ cup sprouts

How to prepare:

1. Add rinsed quinoa to a small pot over medium heat.
2. Stir cook for 2 minutes then add water.
3. Cook it to a boil then reduce to a simmer.
4. Continue cooking for 20 minutes until water is completely absorbed.
5. Now, preheat the oven to 375 degrees F.
6. Spread the beets and carrots on a baking sheet.
7. Drizzle oil and seasonings, toss well to coat.
8. Roast the veggies for 20 minutes.
9. Meanwhile, prepare the tahini dressing by mixing all of its ingredients.
10. Spread the kale on the serving platter.
11. Top them with avocado, tomatoes, quinoa, vegetables, and other toppings.
12. Serve.

Nutritional Values:
- Calories 361
- Total Fat 16.3 g
- Saturated Fat 4.9 g
- Cholesterol 114 mg
- Sodium 515 mg
- Total Carbs 29.3 g
- Fiber 0.1 g
- Sugar 18.2 g
- Protein 3.3 g

French-Style Potato Salad

Preparation time: 10 minutes
Cooking time: 15 minutes
Total time: 25 minutes
Servings: 14

Ingredients:

Potatoes + Vegetables

- 2 lb baby yellow potatoes
- 1 pinch sea salt
- 1 pinch black pepper
- 1 tbsp apple cider vinegar
- 1 cup green onion, diced
- 1/4 cup fresh parsley, chopped

Dressing

- 2 1/2 tbsp spicy brown mustard
- 3 cloves garlic, minced
- 1/4 tsp sea salt

- 1/4 tsp black pepper
- 3 tbsp red wine vinegar
- 1 tbsp apple cider vinegar
- 3 tbsp olive oil
- 1/4 cup fresh dill, chopped

How to prepare:

1. Slice the scrubbed potatoes into ¼-inch slices.
2. Place the slices in a saucepan and pour in water along with a dash of salt.
3. Boil the potatoes and cook for 15 minutes until soft.
4. Drain the potatoes and rinse under cold water.
5. Add the drained potatoes to a serving bowl and season with black pepper, salt, and apple cider vinegar.
6. Now, whisk the remaining ingredients to prepare the dressing in a bowl.
7. Add this dressing to the cooked potatoes and mix well.
8. Serve.

Nutritional Values:

- Calories 205
- Total Fat 22.7 g
- Saturated Fat 6.1 g
- Cholesterol 4 mg
- Sodium 227 mg
- Total Carbs 26.1 g
- Fiber 1.4 g
- Sugar 0.9 g
- Protein 5.2 g

Squash, Pecan, & Pomegranate Salad

Preparation time: 10 minutes
Cooking time: 40 minutes
Total time: 50 minutes
Servings: 6

Ingredients:

Vegetables

- 5 cups butternut squash, peeled & cubed
- 1 tbsp coconut oil; 1 tbsp coconut sugar
- 1 pinch cayenne pepper; 1 pinch sea salt
- 1/2 tsp ground cinnamon
- 2 tbsp maple syrup

Nuts

- 1 cup raw pecans; 2 tsp coconut oil
- 1 tbsp maple syrup; 1 tbsp coconut sugar
- 1 pinch cayenne pepper; 1 pinch sea salt
- 1/2 tsp ground cinnamon

Pomegranate Dressing

- 1/4 cup pomegranate molasses
- 2 cups organic arugula or mixed greens
- 1/2 medium lemon, juiced; 2 tsp olive oil
- 1 pinch sea salt; 1 pinch black pepper
- 1/2 cup pomegranate arils; 1/4 cup red onion, thinly sliced

How to prepare:

1. Start by preheating the oven to 375 degrees F.
2. Spread the potatoes and squash on a baking tray.
3. Toss in coconut oil, salt, maple syrup, cayenne, and sugar.
4. Bake for 20 minutes then remove the squash leaving the potato.
5. Continue cooking for another 5 minutes or more until potato is al dente.
6. Remove the veggies from the tray and transfer to a bowl.
7. Spread pecans in a separate baking tray and roast them for 13 minutes in the oven.
8. Meanwhile, prepare the molasses by heating the pomegranate juice in a saucepan until reduced to 1/4 cup.
9. Toss the potato, squash, and pecan in a salad bowl.
10. Drizzle molasses on top.
11. Garnish as desired.
12. Serve.

Nutritional Values:

- Calories 201
- Total Fat 8.9 g
- Saturated Fat 4.5 g
- Cholesterol 57 mg
- Sodium 340 mg
- Total Carbs 24.7 g
- Fiber 1.2 g
- Sugar 1.3 g
- Protein 15.3 g

Chapter 4. Pasta & Noodles Dishes

Garlic & White Wine Pasta

Preparation time: 10 minutes
Cooking time: 20 minutes
Total time: 30 minutes
Servings: 4

Ingredients:

Brussels Sprouts

- 16 oz Brussels sprouts, halved; 1-2 tbsp olive oil
- 1 pinch sea salt; 1/4 tsp black pepper

Pasta

- 3 tbsp olive oil; 4 large cloves garlic, chopped
- 1/3 cup dry white wine
- 4 tbsp arrowroot starch; 1 3/4 cup almond milk
- 4 tbsp nutritional yeast; Sea salt and black pepper, to taste
- 1/4 cup vegan parmesan cheese; 10 oz vegan, gluten-free pasta

For Serving

- Garlic bread; Simple green salad

How to prepare:

1. Start by preheating the oven to 400 degrees F.
2. Spread the Brussels sprouts on a baking sheet.
3. Add oil, salt, and black pepper then give it a toss.
4. Now, boil the pasta in a pot filled with water until al dente then drain.
5. Now, heat oil in a rimmed skillet over medium heat.
6. Add garlic and sauté for 3 minutes until golden.
7. Stir in white wine and cook for 2 minutes.
8. Whisk in arrowroot and almond milk.
9. Mix well then blend with vegan parmesan cheese, salt, and pepper in a food processor.
10. Heat the almond milk sauce in a skillet over medium heat until it bubbles.
11. Bake the Brussels sprouts in the oven for 15 minutes until golden.
12. Toss the drained pasta with cheese sauce and Brussels sprouts in a large bowl.
13. Mix well and serve.

Nutritional Values:

- Calories 248
- Total Fat 15.7 g
- Saturated Fat 2.7 g
- Cholesterol 75 mg
- Sodium 94 mg
- Total Carbs 31.4 g
- Fiber 0.4 g
- Sugar 3.1 g
- Protein 4.9 g

Eggplant Vegan Pasta

Preparation time: 10 minutes
Cooking time: 20 minutes
Total time: 30 minutes
Servings: 4

Ingredients:

- 12 oz dry pasta
- 1/2 small eggplant, cubed
- 2 cups cremini mushrooms, sliced
- 3 cloves garlic, minced
- 1 1/2 cups vegan marinara sauce
- 2 cups water
- 2 tsp sea salt
- 1 tsp ground black pepper
- 3 tbsp olive oil
- Fresh parsley or basil

How to prepare:

1. Place the eggplant in a colander and sprinkle salt on top.
2. Let them rest for 30 minutes and rinse thoroughly.
3. Now, place a saucepan over medium-high heat.
4. Add eggplant along with olive oil and 1/3 minced garlic, and ½ teaspoon salt.
5. Stir cook for 6 minutes until golden brown then toss in mushrooms.
6. Sauté for 2 minutes approximately then transfer to a bowl.
7. Cook pasta with water, remaining garlic, and marinara sauce in a saucepan.
8. Add salt and black pepper to pasta to adjust seasoning.
9. After cooking it to a boil let it simmer for 10 minutes until pasta is al dente.
10. Toss in the eggplant mixture then garnish as desired.
11. Serve.

Nutritional Values:

- Calories 246
- Total Fat 14.8 g
- Saturated Fat 0.7 g
- Cholesterol 22 mg
- Sodium 220 mg
- Total Carbs 40.3 g
- Fiber 2.4 g
- Sugar 1.2 g
- Protein 2.4 g

Tomato Pesto Pasta

Preparation time: 10 minutes
Cooking time: 10 minutes
Total time: 20 minutes
Servings: 3

Ingredients:

- 10 oz gluten-free pasta
- 3 oz sun-dried tomatoes
- ¼ cup olive oil
- 1 cup fresh basil
- 4 cloves garlic
- 2 tbsp vegan parmesan cheese

How to prepare:

1. Start by boiling the water with salt in a saucepan.
2. Add pasta and cook until al dente then drain.
3. Take a blender jug and add basil, garlic, vegan parmesan, olive oil, and tomatoes.
4. Blend well until it forms a puree to form the pesto.
5. Toss the cooked pasta with pesto in a salad bowl.
6. Top with parmesan and olive oil.
7. Mix well and serve.

Nutritional Values:

- Calories 338
- Total Fat 3.8 g
- Saturated Fat 0.7 g
- Cholesterol 22 mg
- Sodium 620 mg
- Total Carbs 58.3 g
- Fiber 2.4 g
- Sugar 1.2 g
- Protein 5.4 g

Alfredo with Peas

Preparation time: 10 minutes
Cooking time: 10 minutes
Total time: 20 minutes
Servings: 4

Ingredients:

- 2 tbsp extra virgin olive oil
- 3 cloves garlic, minced
- 4 tbsp all-purpose flour
- ¾ cup 2% milk
- 1 cup vegetable stock
- 1 tbsp pesto
- ¼ tsp salt
- ¼ tsp black pepper
- ½ cup freshly grated vegan parmesan cheese
- 1 cup green peas
- ¾ box whole grain pasta

How to prepare:

1. Start by cooking the pasta as per the given instructions on the box then drain.
2. Place a saucepan over medium heat then add garlic along with olive oil.
3. Sauté for 1 minute then add flour while constantly whisking.
4. After 1 minute, add vegetable stock and milk.
5. Mix well until smooth then add pesto, black pepper, parmesan cheese, and salt.
6. Continue cooking until the mixture bubbles.
7. Toss in peas and pasta.
8. Mix well and serve.

Nutritional Values:

- Calories 438
- Total Fat 4.8 g
- Saturated Fat 1.7 g
- Cholesterol 12 mg
- Sodium 520 mg
- Total Carbs 52.3 g
- Fiber 2.3 g
- Sugar 1.2 g
- Protein 2.1 g

Eggplant Parmesan Pasta

Preparation time: 10 minutes
Cooking time: 55 minutes
Total time: 65 minutes
Servings: 2

Ingredients:

Eggplant Parmesan

- 1 medium eggplant
- 1/4 cup unbleached all-purpose flour
- 1 cup panko bread crumbs
- 2 tbsp vegan parmesan
- 1 tsp dried oregano
- 1/4 tsp sea salt
- 1/2 cup almond milk
- 1 tsp cornstarch

Pasta

- 8 oz pasta
- 2 cups marinara sauce

How to prepare:

1. Start by slicing the eggplant into ½-inch thick rounds.
2. Place them in a colander and sprinkle salt over the eggplant.
3. Let them rest for 15 minutes then squeeze the excess water out using a dish towel.
4. Prepare a baking tray by lining it with an aluminum foil.
5. Preheat the oven at 400 degrees F.
6. Boil the pasta as per the given instructions on the box.
7. Now, mix almond milk with salt, oregano, vegan parmesan, and cornstarch in a bowl until smooth.
8. Dip the eggplant in the flour then in the almond milk mixture and then breadcrumbs.
9. Place the coated slices in the baking tray.
10. Bake the eggplant for 30 minutes.
11. Meanwhile, warm up 2 tablespoons oil in a skillet and sear the baked slices in batches until golden on both sides.
12. Warm the marinara in a pan and spread over the cooked pasta.
13. Place the eggplant slices on top.
14. Garnish as desired.
15. Serve.

Nutritional Values:

- Calories 378
- Total Fat 13.8 g
- Saturated Fat 0.7 g
- Cholesterol 2 mg
- Sodium 620 mg
- Total Carbs 43.3 g
- Fiber 2.4 g
- Sugar 1.2 g
- Protein 5.4 g

Green Chili Mac 'N' Cheese

Preparation time: 10 minutes
Cooking time: 27 minutes
Total time: 37 minutes
Servings: 4

Ingredients:

- 10 oz large macaroni shells
- 1/2 medium white onion, diced
- 3-4 cloves garlic, minced
- 1 cup raw cashews
- 1 1/2 cups vegetable broth
- 1 tbsp cornstarch
- 1/2 tsp cumin; 3/4 tsp chili powder
- 2 tbsp nutritional yeast
- 1 4-oz can dice chills
- 1 cup tortilla chips
- Fresh cilantro

How to prepare:

1. Finely crush the tortilla chips to get the crumbs.
2. Spread the crumbs on a baking sheet lined with parchment sheet.
3. Season with salt and avocado oil then toss well to evenly coat.
4. Bake the chips for 10 minutes in an oven at 350 degrees F until golden.
5. Meanwhile, cook the macaroni as per the given instructions on the box and set aside.
6. Take a medium skillet and place over medium low heat.
7. Stir in garlic, olive oil, and onion to the skillet.
8. Sauté for 7 minutes then set it aside.
9. Transfer this garlic mixture to a blender along with remaining ingredients except for the tortilla chips and half of the green chilies.
10. Blend this mixture until smooth then transfer to a bowl.
11. Toss drained pasta with cashew cheese blend.
12. Garnish with reserved chilies and tortilla chips.
13. Serve.

Nutritional Values:

- Calories 304
- Total Fat 30.6 g
- Saturated Fat 13.1 g
- Cholesterol 131 mg
- Sodium 834 mg
- Total Carbs 21.4 g
- Fiber 0.2 g
- Sugar 0.3 g
- Protein 4.6 g

3-Color Pasta

Preparation time: 10 minutes
Cooking time: 10 minutes
Total time: 20 minutes
Servings: 1

Ingredients:

- 1 medium carrot
- 1 small-medium zucchini
- 2 oz whole-wheat spaghetti
- 1/3-1/2 cup tomato sauce
- 3 tbsp sundried tomato spread
- Vegan parmesan cheese
- Fresh basil

How to prepare:

1. Start by cooking the noodles as per the given instructions on the box until al dente.
2. Pass the zucchini and carrot through a spiralizer to get the noodles.
3. Heat the tomato spread with tomato sauce in a pan.
4. Boil the carrot and zucchini noodle in the pasta water for 4 minutes until al dente.
5. Drain and toss the veggies with cooked pasta noodles and tomato mixture in a bowl.
6. Garnish as desired.
7. Serve.

Nutritional Values:

- Calories 341
- Total Fat 4 g
- Saturated Fat 0.5 g
- Cholesterol 69 mg
- Sodium 547 mg
- Total Carbs 36.4 g
- Fiber 1.2 g
- Sugar 1 g
- Protein 10.3 g

Caramelized Onion Mac 'N' Cheese

Preparation time: 10 minutes
Cooking time: 12 minutes
Total time: 22 minutes
Servings: 4

Ingredients:

Pasta

- 1 small-medium eggplant; 1 tbsp olive oil
- 1 1/2 yellow onions, sliced
- 10 oz macaroni noodles
- 4 tbsp nutritional yeast
- 1 3/4 cups almond milk
- 2 tsp garlic powder
- 1 tbsp cornstarch
- Sea salt

Topping

- 1/4 cup panko bread crumbs; 1 tbsp olive oil

How to prepare:

1. Slice the eggplant into ½ inch thick rounds.
2. Place them in a colander then sprinkle salt over the eggplant.
3. Let them sit for 20 minutes until the water is fully drained (squeeze out any excess).
4. Add olive oil along with onions to a skillet placed over medium heat.
5. Stir cook for 12 minutes until caramelized then transfer to a bowl.
6. Set your oven at high broil mode and place a rack in the top portion.
7. Cook the pasta in water until al dente then drain.
8. Spread the eggplant on a baking sheet then broil for 4 minutes.
9. Set them aside covered with a foil for 5 minutes then peel their skin off.
10. Blend the eggplant slices with garlic powder, salt, cornstarch, yeast, and almond milk in a food processor.
11. Once its smooth, transfer to a bowl.
12. Heat the eggplant sauce in a pan for 5 minutes.
13. Toss in noodles along with caramelized onions.
14. Divide the mixture in the serving bowls and garnish with bread crumbs.
15. Serve.

Nutritional Values:

- Calories 248
- Total Fat 15.7 g
- Saturated Fat 2.7 g
- Cholesterol 75 mg
- Sodium 94 mg
- Total Carbs 40.4 g
- Fiber 0.1 g
- Sugar 0.3 g
- Protein 4.9 g

Cheesy Garlic Pasta with Ciabatta

Preparation time: 10 minutes
Cooking time: 10 minutes
Total time: 20 minutes
Servings: 4

Ingredients:

Alfredo Sauce

- 1 tbsp extra virgin olive oil
- 3 cloves garlic, minced
- 1 cup low-fat milk
- 1/2 cup veggie broth
- 2-4 tbsp flour
- 1/4 tsp salt
- 1/4 tsp black pepper
- 1/4 cup grated parmesan cheese
- 1 tbsp pesto
- 1 healthy pinch red pepper flakes
- 10-12 oz pasta, boiled

Cheesy Garlic Ciabatta Bread

- 1 ciabatta bread roll; 2 tbsp butter
- 1 tsp garlic powder; 1 sprinkle mozzarella and parmesan cheese

How to prepare:

1. Start by preheating the oven to 400 degrees F.
2. Place a large saucepan over medium heat then add garlic and olive oil.
3. Sauté until golden then add broth and milk.
4. Mix well then add flour with constant mixing until smooth.
5. Toss in cheese, pesto, red pepper flakes, black pepper, and salt then mix well.
6. Stir cook for 5 minutes then set it aside.
7. Cook the pasta to a boil until al dente then drain.
8. Slice the ciabatta roll in half then butter them.
9. Further cut the roll into strips and place them on a baking sheet.
10. Sprinkle mozzarella, garlic powder, and parmesan over the strips.
11. Toast them for approximately 5 minutes in the oven.
12. Toss the pasta with prepared sauce in a large bowl.
13. Garnish with bread strips.
14. Serve.

Nutritional Values:

- Calories 301
- Total Fat 12.2 g
- Saturated Fat 2.4 g
- Cholesterol 110 mg
- Sodium 276 mg
- Total Carbs 5 g
- Fiber 0.9 g
- Sugar 1.4 g
- Protein 28.8 g

Tomato Red Lentil Pasta

Preparation time: 10 minutes
Cooking time: 30 minutes
Total time: 40 minutes
Servings: 6

Ingredients:

- ¼ cup extra virgin olive oil
- 1 sweet onion, chopped
- 6 cloves garlic, minced
- 1 tbsp dried basil; 1 tbsp dried oregano
- 2 tsp ground turmeric
- Kosher salt and black pepper, to taste
- 1 28-oz can fire-roasted tomatoes
- ½ cup oil-packed sundried tomatoes, chopped
- 1 tbsp apple cider vinegar
- 1 (8-oz) box red lentil pasta
- 2 large handfuls baby spinach

How to prepare:

1. Start by warming up the olive oil in a large pot over medium heat.
2. Add onion and sauté for 10 minutes approximately.
3. Stir in black pepper, salt, turmeric, oregano, basil, and garlic.
4. Sauté for 1 minute then toss tomatoes along with its juices, sundried tomatoes, and vinegar.
5. Cook for 15 minutes on a simmer then blend using an immersion blender.
6. Toss spinach into the sauce and mix well to cook for another 5 minutes.
7. Boil the pasta as per the given instructions on the box then drain.
8. Serve pasta with spinach mixture on top.
9. Garnish as desired.
10. Serve.

Nutritional Values:

- Calories 248
- Total Fat 2.4 g
- Saturated Fat 0.1 g
- Cholesterol 320 mg
- Sodium 350 mg
- Total Carbs 32.2 g
- Fiber 0.7 g
- Sugar 0.7 g
- Protein 44.3 g

Chapter 5. Stir-fried, Grilled & Hashed Vegetables

Grilled Vegetables

Preparation time: 10 minutes
Cooking time: 10 minutes
Total time: 20 minutes
Servings: 6

Ingredients:

- 3 red bell peppers, seeded and halved
- 3 yellow squash, julienned
- 3 zucchinis, sliced into rectangles
- 3 Japanese eggplant, sliced into rectangles
- 1 onion, sliced
- 12 cremini mushrooms
- 1 bunch (1 lb) asparagus, trimmed
- 12 green onions, roots cut off

- 1/4 cup + 2 tbsp olive oil
- Salt and freshly ground black pepper, to taste
- 3 tbsp balsamic vinegar
- 2 garlic cloves, minced
- 1 tsp parsley leaves, chopped
- 1 tsp fresh basil leaves, chopped
- 1/2 tsp fresh rosemary leaves, chopped

How to prepare:

1. Start by preparing and preheating the grill over medium heat.
2. Toss all the veggies with spices, herbs, and oil in a large bowl.
3. Grease the grilling grates and spread the veggies on the grill.
4. Use a tong to flip the veggies.
5. Grill all the veggies until they are slightly charred.
6. Serve warm.

Nutritional Values:
- Calories 372
- Total Fat 11.1 g
- Saturated Fat 5.8 g
- Cholesterol 610 mg
- Sodium 749 mg
- Total Carbs 16.9 g
- Fiber 0.2 g
- Sugar 0.2 g
- Protein 13.5 g

Mixed Vegetable Platter

Preparation time: 10 minutes
Cooking time: 10 minutes
Total time: 20 minutes
Servings: 6

Ingredients:

- 1/4 cup olive oil
- 2 tbsp maple syrup
- 4 tsp balsamic vinegar
- 1 tsp dried oregano
- 1/2 tsp garlic powder
- 1/8 tsp pepper; Salt, to taste
- 1 medium red onion, cut into wedges
- 1 lb fresh asparagus, trimmed
- 3 small carrots, cut in half
- 1 large sweet red pepper, cut into strips
- 1 medium yellow summer squash, cut into slices

How to prepare:

1. Start by whisking the first 7 ingredients in a bowl.
2. Add 3 tablespoons of this marinade to a plastic bag.
3. Toss in all the veggies to the plastic bag then seal it.
4. Shake the bag well then marinate for 2 hours.
5. Preheat a grill over medium heat and grease its grilling grates.
6. Grill the marinated veggies for 4 minutes per side until crispy
7. Garnish with remaining marinade.
8. Serve.

Nutritional Values:

- Calories 114
- Total Fat 5.7 g
- Saturated Fat 2.7 g
- Cholesterol 75 mg
- Sodium 94 mg
- Total Carbs 31.4 g
- Fiber 0.6 g
- Sugar 15 g
- Protein 4.1 g

Grilled Chopped Veggies

Preparation time: 10 minutes
Cooking time: 10 minutes
Total time: 20 minutes
Servings: 4

Ingredients:

- 1 red pepper, sliced
- 1 orange bell pepper, sliced
- 1 green bell pepper, sliced
- 1 zucchini squash, sliced
- 1 red onion, quartered
- 12 oz baby portobello mushrooms
- 1 pinch salt; 1 pinch black pepper
- 1 loaf sourdough bread, sliced
- 3 tbsp olive oil
- 4 garlic cloves, minced
- Fresh basil and oregano for garnish

Vinaigrette

- 3 tbsp red wine vinegar
- 1/4 cup fresh basil, chopped
- 2 garlic cloves, minced; 1 1/2 tbsp maple syrup
- 1 tsp Dijon mustard; 1/4 tsp salt
- 1/4 tsp black pepper; 1/4 tsp red pepper flakes
- 1/3 cup olive oil

How to prepare:

1. Make basil vinaigrette by whisking together all ingredients then set aside.
2. Preheat the grill over high heat.
3. Slice the bread into slices and brush them with a mixture of olive oil and garlic.
4. Season the vegetables with salt and black pepper.
5. Grill the veggies on the hot grill for 3 minutes per side then transfer them to a sheet pan.
6. Grill the bread slices for 2 minutes per side.
7. Chop the cooked veggies and add them to a bowl.
8. Toss in basil vinaigrette and mix well.
9. Garnish with oregano and basil.
10. Serve with grilled bread.

Nutritional Values:

- Calories 249
- Total Fat 11.9 g
- Saturated Fat 1.7 g
- Cholesterol 78 mg
- Sodium 79 mg
- Total Carbs 41.8 g
- Fiber 1.1 g
- Sugar 0.3 g
- Protein 1 g

Garlic Grilled Vegetables

Preparation time: 10 minutes
Cooking time: 15 minutes
Total time: 25 minutes
Servings: 6

Ingredients:

- 1 ear corn, cut into chunks
- 1 medium red onion, wedged
- 1 small green bell pepper, diced
- 1 small red bell pepper, diced
- 1 small yellow bell pepper, diced
- 1 small yellow squash, sliced
- 1 cup mushroom halves
- 2 tbsp oil
- 1 tbsp garlic & herb seasoning

How to prepare:

1. Start by tossing the vegetables with seasonings and oil in a bowl.
2. Thread the veggies on skewers.
3. Prepare and preheat the grill over medium heat.
4. Grill the skewers for 15 minutes while rotating occasionally.
5. Serve warm.

Nutritional Values:

- Calories 213
- Total Fat 14 g
- Saturated Fat 8 g
- Cholesterol 81 mg
- Sodium 162 mg
- Total Carbs 53 g
- Fiber 0.7 g
- Sugar 19 g
- Protein 12 g

Marinated BBQ Vegetables

Preparation time: 10 minutes
Cooking time: 10 minutes
Total time: 20 minutes
Servings: 6

Ingredients:

Vegetables

- 2 red bell peppers, sliced
- 2 yellow bell peppers, sliced; 2 red onions, sliced
- 1 eggplant, cut into 1/2-inch thick semi-circles
- 2 zucchinis, 1/3-inch thick slices
- 2 bunches asparagus, trimmed; 7 oz button mushrooms

Grilling

- 1/4 cup olive oil; 1 tsp salt
- 1 tsp black pepper
- 3 cloves garlic, minced
- 1/4 cup parsley, chopped

Dressing

- 1/3 cup lemon juice
- 1/3 cup olive oil
- 2 tsp white sugar
- 1/2 tsp salt
- 1/2 tsp black pepper
- 2 garlic cloves, minced
- 1/2 tsp dried basil
- 1/2 tsp parsley
- 1/2 tsp oregano
- 1/2 tsp thyme
- 1 tsp chili flake

How to prepare:

1. Prepare the dressing by mixing all of its ingredients in a bowl.
2. Cut all the veggies into large pieces and wedges.
3. Toss the veggies with grilling seasonings in a bowl.
4. Grill each vegetable for 2-4 minutes per side until slightly charred.
5. Toss the veggies with the prepared marinade.
6. Serve warm.

Nutritional Values:

- Calories 379
- Total Fat 29.7 g
- Saturated Fat 18.6 g
- Cholesterol 141 mg
- Sodium 193 mg
- Total Carbs 23.7g
- Fiber 0.9 g
- Sugar 1.3 g
- Protein 5.2 g

Stir-Fry Vegetables

Preparation time: 10 minutes
Cooking time: 9 minutes
Total time: 19 minutes
Servings: 10

Ingredients:

- 1 tbsp oil
- 1 medium onion, sliced
- 1 cup carrots, sliced
- 2 cups broccoli florets
- 2 cups sugar snap peas
- 1 large red bell pepper, cut strips
- 1 tbsp reduced-sodium soy sauce
- 1 tsp garlic powder
- 1 tsp ginger, ground
- 2 tsp sesame seed, toasted

How to prepare:

1. Start by preheating the oil in a deep skillet over medium-high heat.
2. Toss in carrots and onions, sauté for 2 minutes.
3. Stir in remaining ingredients and stir cook for 7 minutes.
4. Add garlic powder, ginger, and soy sauce.
5. Garnish with sesame seeds.
6. Serve.

Nutritional Values:

- Calories 268
- Total Fat 6 g
- Saturated Fat 1.2 g
- Cholesterol 351 mg
- Sodium 103 mg
- Total Carbs 12.8 g
- Fiber 9.2 g
- Sugar 2.9 g
- Protein 7.2 g

Chinese Vegetable Stir-Fry

Preparation time: 10 minutes
Cooking time: 10 minutes
Total time: 20 minutes
Servings: 4

Ingredients:

- 1/3 cup soy sauce; 3 tbsp water
- 2 tbsp dry sherry
- 1 tsp Asian sesame oil; 2 tsp sugar
- 1 tbsp cornstarch
- 1/4 tsp red pepper flakes
- 1/4 tsp dry mustard; 2 tbsp vegetable oil
- 1 lb broccoli, cut into florets
- 7 oz shiitake mushrooms, thinly sliced
- 1 red bell pepper, thinly sliced
- 3 cloves garlic, finely chopped
- 3 scallions, thinly sliced
- 1 tbsp grated fresh ginger

How to prepare:

1. Start by whisking water, soy sauce, sesame oil, red pepper flakes, mustard, cornstarch, sugar, sesame oil, and dry sherry in a small bowl.
2. Place a nonstick skillet filled with water up to 1 inch on medium heat.
3. Toss in broccoli then cook for 3 minutes and drain.
4. Empty the skillet and let it dry.
5. Pour 2 tablespoons oil into the same skillet and heat it.
6. Toss in red pepper and mushrooms, sauté for 6 minutes.
7. Stir in ginger, garlic, and scallions. Stir cook for 30 seconds.
8. Add the drained broccoli to this pan and sauté for 1 minute.
9. Stir in the cornstarch mixture to the broccoli and cook until it thickens.
10. Serve warm.

Nutritional Values:

- Calories 201
- Total Fat 32.2 g
- Saturated Fat 2.4 g
- Cholesterol 110 mg
- Sodium 276 mg
- Total Carbs 25 g
- Fiber 0.9 g
- Sugar 1.4 g
- Protein 8.8 g

Vegetable Satay

Preparation time: 10 minutes
Cooking time: 20 minutes
Total time: 30 minutes
Servings: 4

Ingredients:

- 1 cup vegetable broth
- 1 tbsp cornstarch
- 1 tbsp reduced-sodium soy sauce
- 1 tbsp vegetable oil
- 1 cup broccoli florets
- 1 cup cauliflower florets
- 1 cup baby carrots
- 2 stalks celery, sliced
- 2 tsp grated fresh ginger root
- 1 clove garlic, minced
- ½ tsp sesame seeds

How to prepare:

1. Start by mixing broth with soy sauce and cornstarch in a small bowl until smooth.
2. Place a skillet over medium-high heat and add oil to preheat.
3. Toss in all the vegetables and sauté until tender and crispy.
4. Stir in broth mixture and cook until it boils.
5. Garnish with sesame seeds.
6. Serve warm.

Nutritional Values:

- Calories 219
- Total Fat 19.7 g
- Saturated Fat 18.6 g
- Cholesterol 141 mg
- Sodium 193 mg
- Total Carbs 23.7 g
- Fiber 0.2 g
- Sugar 1.3 g
- Protein 5.2 g

Ginger Vegetable Stir-Fry

Preparation time: 10 minutes
Cooking time: 20 minutes
Total time: 30 minutes
Servings: 6

Ingredients:

- 1 tbsp cornstarch
- 1 1/2 cloves garlic, crushed
- 2 tsp fresh ginger root, chopped
- 1/4 cup vegetable oil, divided
- 1 small head broccoli, cut into florets
- 1/2 cup snow peas
- 3/4 cup carrots, julienned
- 1/2 cup green beans, halved
- 2 tbsp soy sauce
- 2 1/2 tbsp water
- 1/4 cup chopped onion
- 1/2 tbsp salt

How to prepare:

1. Start by tossing all the ingredients in a large bowl.
2. Place a suitable skillet over medium heat and add the seasoned vegetables.
3. Stir cook until all the veggies are soft, tender and crispy.
4. Serve.

Nutritional Values:

- Calories 248
- Total Fat 15.7 g
- Saturated Fat 2.7 g
- Cholesterol 75 mg
- Sodium 94 mg
- Total Carbs 38.4 g
- Fiber 0.3 g
- Sugar 0.1 g
- Protein 14.1 g

Winter Vegetable Hash

Preparation time: 10 minutes
Cooking time: 30 minutes
Total time: 40 minutes
Servings: 6

Ingredients:

- 3 tbsp olive oil
- 2 tbsp butter
- 1 lb Yukon gold potatoes, diced
- 1/2 lb fresh shiitake mushrooms, diced
- 1 red bell pepper, diced
- 1 small acorn squash, diced
- 1 shallot, finely chopped
- 2 tsp garlic powder
- 1 pinch salt
- 1 pinch ground black pepper
- 1 cup chopped kale
- 4 sprigs fresh sage

How to prepare:

1. Add both butter and oil to a large skillet placed over medium heat.
2. Toss in all the veggies along with seasonings, except sage and kale.
3. Stir cook for 25 minutes until soft and tender.
4. Add the sage and kale then sauté for 5 minutes.
5. Serve.

Nutritional Values:

- Calories 301
- Total Fat 12.2 g
- Saturated Fat 2.4 g
- Cholesterol 110 mg
- Sodium 276 mg
- Total Carbs 12.5 g
- Fiber 0.9 g
- Sugar 1.4 g
- Protein 8.8 g

Chapter 6. Desserts & Snacks

Hawaiian Shaved Ice

Preparation time: 10 minutes
Cooking time: 0 minutes
Total time: 10 minutes
Servings: 2

Ingredients:

- 1 cup sugar
- 1 qt strawberries, diced
- 1½ cups mango juice
- 1 mango, diced
- ½ cup toasted coconut

How to prepare:

1. Start by adding 1 cup water along with ¾ cup sugar to a medium pot.
2. Let this sugar water cook to a boil then remove from the heat.
3. Stir in 2 cups of water and mix well.
4. Pour this mixture into a shallow dish and spread it evenly.
5. Freeze it for 5 hours while stirring every 45 minutes to get crystal ice.
6. Blend the strawberries with the remaining sugar in a blender until smooth.
7. Divide the ice into the serving glasses and top it with mango and strawberries mixture.
8. Garnish with coconut and mango.
9. Serve.

Nutritional Values:

- Calories 398
- Total Fat 6 g
- Saturated Fat 7 g
- Cholesterol 632 mg
- Sodium 497 mg
- Total Carbs 91 g
- Fiber 3 g
- Sugar 83 g
- Protein 2 g

Butterscotch Tart

Preparation time: 10 minutes
Cooking time: 40 minutes
Total time: 50 minutes
Servings: 10

Ingredients:

Crust

- ½ cup granulated sugar
- ¼ cup virgin coconut oil; 1 tsp pure vanilla extract
- 2 cups almond meal flour; ½ tsp salt

Filling

- ⅔ cup packed light brown sugar
- ⅔ cup canned coconut cream
- ½ cup coconut oil
- 1 tsp kosher salt
- Flaked sea salt, as needed
- 1 Granny Smith apple, sliced

How to prepare:

1. Start by preheating the oven to 375 degrees F.
2. Prepare the crust by blending all its ingredients in a blender until smooth.
3. Spread this batter in a 9-inch tart pan evenly.
4. Freeze this batter for 10 minutes then bake for 15 minutes until golden brown.
5. Now, prepare the filling by heating its ingredients in a saucepan.
6. Cook this mixture for 25 minutes until it thickens then allow it to cool.
7. Add this filling to the tart then refrigerate for 2 hours.
8. Serve.

Nutritional Values:

- Calories 132
- Total Fat 8.9 g
- Saturated Fat 4.5 g
- Cholesterol 57 mg
- Sodium 340 mg
- Total Carbs 24.7 g
- Fiber 1.2 g
- Sugar 12.3 g
- Protein 5.3 g

4-Ingredient Brownies

Preparation time: 10 minutes
Cooking time: 15 minutes
Total time: 25 minutes
Servings: 12

Ingredients:

- 2 cups dates, pitted
- ¼ cup warm water
- ½ cup salted peanut butter
- 2 tbsp melted coconut oil
- 1/3 cup cocoa powder
- 1/3 cup dark chocolate chips
- ½ cup raw walnuts, chopped

How to prepare:

1. Start by preheating the oven to 350 degrees F. Layer a loaf pan with a parchment sheet.
2. Blend the pitted dates in the food processor until it turns into a fine mixture.
3. Add hot water to the processor and blend while scraping down from the sides.
4. Now, add cacao powder, coconut oil, and peanut butter then blend again.
5. Fold in walnuts and chocolate chips.
6. Mix well then spread this mixture in the loaf pan.
7. Bake the dates batter for 15 minutes in the oven.
8. Serve chilled.

Nutritional Values:

- Calories 427
- Total Fat 31.1 g
- Saturated Fat 4.2 g
- Cholesterol 123 mg
- Sodium 86 mg
- Total Carbs 9 g
- Sugar 12.4 g
- Fiber 19.8 g
- Protein 3.5 g

Vegan Lemon Cake

Preparation time: 20 minutes
Chilling time: 5 hours
Total time: 5 hours 10 minutes
Servings: 10

Ingredients:

Crust

- 2½ cups pecans; 1 cup pitted dates
- 2 tbsp maple syrup

Filling

- 3 cups prepared cauliflower rice
- 3 avocados, halved and pitted
- 1½ cups pineapple, crushed
- ¾ cup maple syrup
- 1 lemon , zest and juice
- ½ tsp pure vanilla extract
- ½ tsp lemon extract
- 1 pinch cinnamon

Topping

- 1½ cups plain coconut yogurt
- 1 tsp pure vanilla extract; 3 tbsp maple syrup

How to prepare:

1. Layer a 9-inch springform pan with a parchment sheet.
2. Add pecans to a food processor and grind until fine.
3. Stir in maple syrup and dates to the pecans and blend for 1 minute.
4. Spread this crust mixture in the prepared pan.

Make the filling:

1. To prepare the filling, blend cauliflower rice with maple syrup, lemon juice, lemon zest, pineapple, and avocados in a food processor.
2. Add cinnamon, lemon extract, and vanilla extract to the processor.
3. Mix well then spread this filling in the crust.
4. Freeze this cake overnight or for at least 5 hours.
5. Prepare the topping by whisking the yogurt with maple syrup and vanilla extract.
6. Spread this mixture over the cake.
7. Slice and serve.

Nutritional Values:

- Calories 398
- Total Fat 13.8 g
- Saturated Fat 5.1 g
- Cholesterol 200 mg
- Sodium 272 mg
- Total Carbs 53.6 g
- Fiber 1 g
- Sugar 12.3 g
- Protein 1.8 g

Baked Sesame Fries

Preparation time: 10 minutes
Cooking time: 25 minutes
Total time: 35 minutes
Servings: 4

Ingredients:

- 1 lb Yukon gold potatoes, unpeeled, cut into wedges
- 1 tbsp avocado oil
- 2 tbsp sesame seeds
- 1 tbsp potato starch
- 1 tbsp nutritional yeast
- Salt, to taste
- Black pepper, to taste

How to prepare:

1. Start by preheating the oven to 425 degrees F. Layer a baking tray with parchment paper.
2. Add the potatoes along with rest of the ingredients to the baking sheet.
3. Toss well then bake for 25 minutes, flipping halfway through.
4. Serve warm.

Nutritional Values:

- Calories 165
- Total Fat 14 g
- Saturated Fat 7 g
- Cholesterol 632 mg
- Sodium 497 mg
- Total Carbs 6 g
- Fiber 3 g
- Sugar 1 g
- Protein 5 g

Crispy Cauliflower

Preparation time: 10 minutes
Cooking time: 30 minutes
Total time: 40 minutes
Servings: 6

Ingredients:

- 1 head cauliflower, cut into florets
- 2 tbsp potato starch
- 1/2 tsp salt
- 1/4 tsp black pepper
- 1/2 tsp turmeric
- 1 tbsp nutritional yeast, optional
- 1/2 tsp chili powder or paprika
- 1 tbsp avocado oil

How to prepare:

1. Start by preheating the oven to 450 degrees F.
2. Grease a baking sheet with a tablespoon of oil.
3. Add cauliflower to the baking sheet and toss in oil and rest of the ingredients.
4. Mix well then bake for 30 minutes.
5. Serve.

Nutritional Values:

- Calories 172
- Total Fat 11.8 g
- Saturated Fat 4.4 g
- Cholesterol 62 mg
- Sodium 871 mg
- Total Carbs 45.8 g
- Fiber 0.6 g
- Sugar 2.3 g
- Protein 4 g

Spinach Mushroom Pockets

Preparation time: 10 minutes
Cooking time: 23 minutes
Total time: 33 minutes
Servings: 4

Ingredients:

- 1 package puff pastry
- 16 oz mushrooms, sliced
- 2 bags spinach
- 1 1/2 tbsp garlic, minced
- 1 pinch salt
- 1 block extra-firm tofu, pressed
- 1 tsp onion powder
- 1 tsp basil
- 1 tsp oregano
- Black pepper, to taste
- 1/4 tsp salt

- 2 1/2 tbsp nutritional yeast
- 2 tbsp lemon juice
- 1 tsp mustard
- 1 tbsp milk

How to prepare:

1. Place mushrooms in a large pot and heat until they release their liquid.
2. Stir in 1.5 teaspoons garlic and spinach then cover with a lid.
3. Cook for 3 minutes until spinach wilts.
4. Toss rest of the ingredients in a bowl and set it aside.
5. Spread the pastry into a thin sheet and cut circles out of it.
6. Divide the filling in the circles and fold the circle, then pinch the edges closed.
7. Bake them for 20 minutes approximately in the oven at 375 degrees.
8. Serve.

Nutritional Values:

- Calories 246
- Total Fat 7.4 g
- Saturated Fat 4.6 g
- Cholesterol 105 mg
- Sodium 353 mg
- Total Carbs 29.4 g
- Sugar 6.5 g
- Fiber 2.7 g
- Protein 7.2 g

Breaded Tofu

Preparation time: 10 minutes
Cooking time: 10 minutes
Total time: 20 minutes
Servings: 4

Ingredients:

- 1 (14-oz) package extra-firm tofu
- ½ cup cornstarch
- ½ cup breadcrumbs
- ¼ cup of water
- ¼ cup of vegetable oil
- 2 tbsp soy sauce
- 1 tbsp nutritional yeast
- 1 pinch salt
- ½ cup BBQ sauce

How to prepare:

1. Drain the tofu then slice it into finger-length strips.
2. Whisk water, soy sauce, and cornstarch in a small bowl.
3. Mix breadcrumbs with salt and yeast in a shallow bowl.
4. Pour vegetable oil into a large pan and heat over medium-high heat.
5. First, dip the tofu in the cornstarch mixture then coat them with breadcrumbs mixture.
6. Shallow fry the tofu for 3 minutes per side.
7. Serve.

Nutritional Values:

- Calories 293
- Total Fat 16 g
- Saturated Fat 2.3 g
- Cholesterol 75 mg
- Sodium 386 mg
- Total Carbs 25.2 g
- Sugar 2.6 g
- Fiber 1.9 g
- Protein 4.2 g

Raisin Protein Balls

Preparation time: 10 minutes
Freezing time: 30 minutes
Total time: 40 minutes
Servings: 6

Ingredients:

- 1 cup dry oats
- ½ cup creamy peanut butter
- ¼ cup raisins

How to prepare:

1. Start by thoroughly mixing all the ingredients in a bowl.
2. Make golf ball sized fat bombs out of it.
3. Place them on a baking sheet and freeze for 30 minutes.
4. Serve.

Nutritional Values:

- Calories 169
- Total Fat 10.6 g
- Saturated Fat 3.1 g
- Cholesterol 131 mg
- Sodium 834 mg
- Total Carbs 31.4 g
- Fiber 0.2 g
- Sugar 0.3 g
- Protein 4.6 g

Cheese Cucumber Bites

Preparation time: 10 minutes
Cooking time: 0 minutes
Total time: 10 minutes
Servings: 8

Ingredients:

- 4 large cucumbers
- 1 cup raw sunflower seeds
- 1/2 tsp salt
- 2 tbsp raw red onion, chopped
- 1 handful fresh chives, chopped
- 1 clove fresh garlic, chopped
- 2 tbsp nutritional yeast
- 2 tbsp fresh lemon juice
- 1/2 cup water

How to prepare:

1. Start by blending sunflower seeds with salt in a food processor for 20 seconds.
2. Toss in remaining ingredients except for the cucumber and chives and process until smooth.
3. Slice the cucumber into 1.5-inch thick rounds.*
4. Top each slice with sunflower mixture.
5. Garnish with sumac and chives.
6. Serve.

Nutritional Values:

- Calories 211
- Total Fat 25.5 g
- Saturated Fat 12.4 g
- Cholesterol 69 mg
- Sodium 58 mg
- Total Carbs 32.4 g
- Fiber 0.7 g
- Sugar 0.3 g
- Protein 1.4 g

Chapter 7. Homemade Basics, Sauces, and Condiments

Tomatillo Green Salsa

Preparation time: 10 minutes
Cooking time: 7 minutes
Total time: 17 minutes
Servings: 12

Ingredients:

- 8 small tomatillos
- ½ white onion, cut in half
- 1½ tsp garlic, minced
- 1 jalapeño, halved and seeded
- ⅓ cup packed cilantro, chopped
- 1 (4-oz) can mild green chili peppers, chopped

Additions

- ½ tbsp ground cumin
- Salt and pepper, to taste
- Seeds from jalapeño

How to prepare:

1. Start by setting the oven on broil.
2. Layer a baking sheet with aluminum foil.
3. Remove the tomatillos husk then cut them in half.
4. Place the tomatillos and onion on a baking sheet.
5. Top them with jalapenos and garlic then broil for 7 minutes.
6. Transfer to a food processor along with chili peppers and cilantro then blend until chunky.
7. Serve.

Nutritional Information:

- Calories 23
- Total Fat 0.5 g
- Saturated Fat 0 g
- Cholesterol 0mg
- Sodium 488 mg
- Total Carbs 4.3 g
- Sugar 2.6 g
- Fiber 0 g
- Protein 1 g

Thai Peanut Sauce

Preparation time: 10 minutes
Cooking time: 0 minutes
Total time: 10 minutes
Servings: 6

Ingredients:

- 2 tbsp soy sauce
- 1 tbsp rice vinegar
- 1 tsp minced garlic
- 3 tbsp peanut butter
- ¼ cup almond milk
- 1 tsp Thai chili paste

How to prepare:

1. Start by mixing in all the ingredients in a bowl until smooth.
2. Heat this mixture for 30 seconds in the microwave.
3. Serve.

Nutritional Information:

- Calories 12
- Total Fat 0.7 g
- Saturated Fat 0 g
- Cholesterol 2 mg
- Sodium 125 mg
- Total Carbs 1.5 g
- Sugar 0.7 g
- Fiber 0.4 g
- Protein 0.3 g

Tofu Island Dressing

Preparation time: 10 minutes
Cooking time: 0 minutes
Total time: 10 minutes
Servings: 12

Ingredients:

- 1 (12 oz) package extra-firm silken tofu
- 4 dates, pitted
- 1 garlic clove, minced
- ¼ cup red wine vinegar
- ¼ cup tomato purée
- 1 tsp prepared horseradish
- ½ tsp tamari
- ½ tsp mustard powder
- ½ tsp paprika

How to prepare:

1. Start by adding dates and tofu to a blender until smooth.
2. Toss in rest of the ingredients and blend until pureed.
3. Serve.

Nutritional Values:

- Calories 12
- Total Fat 0.1 g
- Saturated Fat 0 g
- Cholesterol 0 mg
- Sodium 86 mg
- Total Carbs 1.2 g
- Sugar 0.3 g
- Fiber 0.2 g
- Protein 0.1 g

Quick Ketchup

Preparation time: 10 minutes
Cooking time: 0 minutes
Total time: 10 minutes
Servings: 8

Ingredients:

- 1 (6 oz) can tomato paste
- ¼ cup filtered water
- 3 tbsp apple cider vinegar
- 1 tbsp balsamic vinegar
- 1 tbsp pure maple syrup
- 1 tsp onion powder
- ½ tsp garlic powder
- ½ tsp sea salt
- ⅛ tsp ground allspice

How to prepare:

1. Start mixing all the sauce ingredients in a mason jar.
2. Cover the sauce and refrigerate.
3. Serve when needed.

Nutritional Values:

- Calories 19
- Total Fat 1.1 g
- Saturated Fat 0.4 g
- Cholesterol 2 mg
- Sodium 84 mg
- Total Carbs 2.1 g
- Sugar 1.3 g
- Fiber 0.3 g
- Protein 0.9 g

Date Purée

Preparation time: 10 minutes
Cooking time: 0 minutes
Total time: 10 minutes
Servings: 8

Ingredients:

- 2 cups Medjool dates, pitted
- 2 cups of water

How to prepare:

1. Add water and pitted dates to a food processor.
2. Blend this date mixture until smooth.
3. Refrigerate.
4. Serve.

Nutritional Values:

- Calories 13
- Total Fat 1.3 g
- Saturated Fat 0.7 g
- Cholesterol 3 mg
- Sodium 48 mg
- Total Carbs 1.8 g
- Sugar 1.6 g
- Fiber 0.1 g
- Protein 0.2 g

Vegan Tzatziki

Preparation time: 10 minutes
Cooking time: 0 minutes
Total time: 10 minutes
Servings: 6

Ingredients:

- 1 English cucumber, grated
- 1 cup non-dairy yogurt
- 2 cloves roasted garlic
- ½ lemon, juiced
- 1 tbsp dill, chopped
- Kosher salt and black pepper, to taste

How to prepare:

1. Start by throwing all the ingredients into a glass bowl.
2. Mix well then refrigerate.
3. Serve.

Nutritional Values:

- Calories 22
- Total Fat 1.5 g
- Saturated Fat 0.6 g
- Cholesterol 3 mg
- Sodium 126 mg
- Total Carbs 6.3 g
- Sugar 5.1 g
- Fiber 0.7 g
- Protein 0.6 g

Jalapeño Dip

Preparation time: 10 minutes
Cooking time: 0 minutes
Total time: 10 minutes
Servings: 12

Ingredients:

- 2 cups cashews, soaked and drained
- 2 lemons, juiced
- 2 1/2 tbsp apple cider vinegar
- 1-2 tbsp sauerkraut
- 1 jalapeño, chopped
- 2 tbsp chives
- 1 tsp onion powder
- 2/3 tsp garlic powder
- 2 tsp black pepper
- 1 tsp salt

How to prepare:

1. Start by throwing all the ingredients to a blender jug.
2. Blend well until smooth.
3. Serve.

Nutritional Values:

- Calories 25
- Total Fat 1.8 g
- Saturated Fat 0.8 g
- Cholesterol 3 mg
- Sodium 537 mg
- Total Carbs 2.5 g
- Sugar 1.7 g
- Fiber 0.5 g
- Protein 0.6 g

Almond Dip

Preparation time: 10 minutes
Cooking time: 0 minutes
Total time: 10 minutes
Servings: 4

Ingredients:

- ½ cup raw almonds
- ½ cup water
- ¼ cup grapeseed oil
- ¼ cup lemon juice
- 3 1/2 tbsp nutritional yeast
- 2 tbsp garlic infused oil
- ¼ tsp salt
- ½ tsp cumin
- ½ tsp chili powder
- ¼ tsp ground coriander
- ¼ tsp paprika
- ¼ tsp cayenne pepper

138

How to prepare:

1. Start by throwing all the ingredients to a blender jug.
2. Blend well until smooth.
3. Serve.

Nutritional Values:

- Calories 13
- Total Fat 0.2 g
- Saturated Fat 0 g
- Cholesterol 0 mg
- Sodium 738 mg
- Total Carbs 11.3 g
- Sugar 0.2 g
- Fiber 0.5 g
- Protein 0.3 g

Chipotle Mayo with Cauliflower

Preparation time: 10 minutes
Cooking time: 18 minutes
Total time: 28 minutes
Servings: 12

Ingredients:

- 3 cups cauliflower florets
- 1 cup vegetable broth
- 1 dried chipotle pepper, seeds removed
- 2 Medjool dates, seed and stem removed
- 1/3 cup shallot, chopped
- 1 tbsp garlic, chopped
- 2 tbsp flaxseed meal
- 1 tbsp Dijon mustard
- 2 tsp white wine vinegar
- 1 tbsp + 1 tsp lime juice
- 1 tsp tamari; 2 tsp paprika
- 2 tsp smoked paprika

How to prepare:

1. Start by steaming the cauliflower florets in a steamer for 10 minutes.
2. Meanwhile, add chipotle to a deep saucepan and stir cook for 2 minutes.
3. Stir in enough water to cover the pepper along with two dates.
4. Cook this mixture to a boil then reduce to a simmer.
5. After 6 minutes, drain the chipotle.
6. Add all the prepared ingredients with spices to a blender until smooth.
7. Serve.

Nutritional Values:

- Calories 10
- Total Fat 0 g
- Saturated Fat 0 g
- Cholesterol 0 mg
- Sodium 205 mg
- Total Carbs 3.3 g
- Sugar 2.7 g
- Fiber 0.1 g
- Protein 0 g

Mango Dipping Sauce

Preparation time: 10 minutes
Cooking time: 0 minutes
Total time: 10 minutes
Servings: 12

Ingredients:

- 1 cup mango
- 2 tbsp tahini
- 2 tbsp apple cider vinegar
- 2 tbsp water
- 2 tbsp ginger minced or whole
- 1 tsp white miso paste

How to prepare:

1. Start by throwing all the ingredients to a blender jug.
2. Blend well until smooth then store.
3. Serve.

Nutritional Values:

- Calories 17
- Total Fat 1 g
- Saturated Fat 0.6 g
- Cholesterol 3 mg
- Sodium 84 mg
- Total Carbs 6.8 g
- Sugar 1.3 g
- Fiber 0.3 g
- Protein 0.9 g

Chapter 8. Drinks
Hibiscus Tea

Preparation time: 10 minutes
Cooking time: 15 minutes
Total time: 25 minutes
Servings: 4

Ingredients:

- ½ cup dried hibiscus flowers
- 4 cups filtered water
- 20 drops liquid stevia

How to prepare:

1. Add half cup of the dried flowers to 4 cups boiling water for 15 minutes.
2. Stir in stevia and mix well.
3. Remove the tea from the heat and allow the mixture to cool.
4. Drain this mixture and refrigerate.
5. Serve.

Nutritional Values:

- Calories 14
- Total Fat 0g
- Saturated Fat 0g
- Cholesterol 0 mg
- Sodium 54 mg
- Total Carbs 14.1 g
- Sugar 0.3 g
- Fiber 0.4 g
- Protein 0.4 g

Turmeric Ginger Tea

Preparation time: 10 minutes
Cooking time: 10 minutes
Total time: 20 minutes
Servings: 2

Ingredients:

- 2 cups water
- 1 tsp turmeric root, grated
- 1 tsp ginger root, grated
- 1/2 tsp ground cinnamon
- 1 tbsp maple syrup

How to prepare:

1. Start by heating the water in a saucepan over medium heat.
2. Stir in ginger, cinnamon, maple syrup, and turmeric root.
3. Mix well and let it simmer for 10 minutes.
4. Strain and serve with ice.

Nutritional Values:

- Calories 80
- Total Fat 1.3 g
- Saturated Fat 0.7 g
- Cholesterol 3 mg
- Sodium 23 mg
- Total Carbs 18.5 g
- Sugar 11.1 g
- Fiber 0.3 g
- Protein 0.3 g

Moroccan Spiced Eggnog

Preparation time: 10 minutes
Chill time: 1 hour
Total time: 1 hour 10 minutes
Servings: 8

Ingredients:

- 8 cups non-dairy milk
- 2 frozen bananas, broken into pieces
- 6 Medjool dates, pitted
- 2 tsp all spice
- 1 tsp ground cinnamon
- 1 tsp ground coriander
- 1/2 tsp nutmeg
- 1/3 tsp ground cloves

How to prepare:

1. Start by throwing all the ingredients into a food processor.
2. Blend well until fully incorporated.
3. Refrigerate for 1 hour then serve.

Nutritional Values:

- Calories 19
- Total Fat 0.4 g
- Saturated Fat 0 g
- Cholesterol 0 mg
- Sodium 52 mg
- Total Carbs 24.8 g
- Sugar 2.4 g
- Fiber 1.4 g
- Protein 0.4 g

Vanilla Soy Eggnog

Preparation time: 10 minutes
Chill time: 1 hour
Total time: 1 hour 10 minutes
Servings: 2

Ingredients:

- 1 qt soy milk
- 6 oz tofu
- 6 tbsp maple syrup
- 1/4 cup brandy
- 2 tsp vanilla
- 1/2 tsp cardamom
- 1/4 tsp nutmeg
- 1/4 tsp cloves ground
- 1/2 tsp cinnamon

How to prepare:

1. Start by throwing all the ingredients into a food processor.
2. Blend well until fully incorporated.
3. Refrigerate for 1 hour then serve.

Nutritional Values:

- Calories 98
- Total Fat 1.5 g
- Saturated Fat 0 g
- Cholesterol 0 mg
- Sodium 94 mg
- Total Carbs 31.5 g
- Sugar 1.3 g
- Fiber 0.1 g
- Protein 10 g

Lemon Mint Beverage

Preparation time: 10 minutes
Chill time: 1 hour
Total time: 1 hour 10 minutes
Servings: 2

Ingredients:

- 25 ml vodka
- 12.5 ml lemon juice
- 12.5 ml simple syrup
- a handful of fresh mint
- 1 drop oregano essential oil

How to prepare:

1. Start by throwing all the ingredients into a food processor.
2. Blend well until fully incorporated.
3. Refrigerate for 1 hour then serve.

Nutritional Values:

- Calories 121
- Total Fat 1.2 g
- Saturated Fat 0.7 g
- Cholesterol 3 mg
- Sodium 84 mg
- Total Carbs 7.5 g
- Sugar 6 g
- Fiber 0.3 g
- Protein 0.6 g

Cinnamon Almond Milk

Preparation time: 10 minutes
Chill time: 4 days
Total time: 4 days and 10 minutes
Servings: 4

Ingredients:

- 1 cup raw almonds, soaked
- 3 1/2 cups filtered water
- 4 pitted Medjool dates
- 1 whole vanilla bean, chopped
- 1/4 tsp cinnamon
- Small pinch fine sea salt

How to prepare:

1. Soak almonds in water overnight then drain.
2. Blend the almonds with pitted dates, vanilla bean, and filtered water in a food processor.
3. Spread a nut milk bag or cheese cloth in a large bowl.
4. Slowly pour in the almond mixture then squeeze the bag to strain the milk.
5. Add salt and cinnamon to the milk then mix well.
6. Pour this milk into a glass jar and seal the jar.
7. Refrigerate for 4 days.
8. Serve.

Nutritional Values:

-   Calories 115
-   Total Fat 1.1 g
-   Saturated Fat 0.4 g
-   Cholesterol 2 mg
-   Sodium 24 mg
-   Total Carbs 24.1 g
-   Sugar 1.3 g
-   Fiber 0.3 g
-   Protein 2.5 g

Mango Lassi

Preparation time: 10 minutes
Chill time: 1 hour
Total time: 1 hour 10 minutes
Servings: 2

Ingredients:

- 1 cup coconut yogurt
- 1 cup mango chunks
- 1/4 cup soy milk
- 2 Medjool dates, pitted

How to prepare:

1. Start by throwing all the ingredients into a food processor.
2. Blend well until fully incorporated.
3. Refrigerate for 1 hour then serve.

Nutritional Values:

- Calories 116
- Total Fat 0.1 g
- Saturated Fat 0g
- Cholesterol 0 mg
- Sodium 144 mg
- Total Carbs 6.1 g
- Sugar 3.5 g
- Fiber 0.1 g
- Protein 0.1 g

Cardamom Turmeric Tea

Preparation time: 10 minutes
Cooking time: 2 minutes
Total time: 12 minutes
Servings: 2

Ingredients:

Chai Spice Tea

- 3 cups water; 1-2 tsp loose tea
- 1/4 tsp chai spice
- 1/2 tsp grated ginger
- 2 tbsp sugar, raw
- 1 tbsp maple syrup

Turmeric milk

- 1 cup coconut milk
- 1/4 tsp turmeric
- 1/4 tsp ground cinnamon
- 1 tbsp sugar, raw

How to prepare:

1. Start by adding tea ingredients to a saucepan then boil for a minute.
2. Reduce it to a simmer and cook for 2 minutes then strain.
3. Stir in remaining ingredients and heat again.
4. Serve.

Nutritional Values:

- Calories 109
- Total Fat 12 g
- Saturated Fat 03 g
- Cholesterol 01 mg
- Sodium 10 mg
- Total Carbs 23.6 g
- Sugar 2 g
- Fiber 0 g
- Protein 10 g

Indian Spiced Buttermilk

Preparation time: 10 minutes
Chill time: 1 hour
Total time: 1 hour 10 minutes
Servings: 2

Ingredients:

- 1 cup nondairy yogurt
- 1 cup cold water
- Ice, as needed
- 1/2 tsp ground cumin
- 2 mint leaves
- 1/4 tsp Indian Sulphur salt
- 1/8 tsp black pepper
- 1 dash lemon juice
- 1/4 tsp ground cumin, for garnish

How to prepare:

1. Start by throwing all the ingredients into a food processor.
2. Blend well until fully incorporated.
3. Refrigerate for 1 hour then serve.

Nutritional Values:

- Calories 97
- Total Fat 14 g
- Saturated Fat 7 g
- Cholesterol 632 mg
- Sodium 497 mg
- Total Carbs 6 g
- Fiber 3 g
- Sugar 1 g
- Protein 5 g

Indian Lemonade

Preparation time: 10 minutes
Chill time: 1 hour
Total time: 1 hour 10 minutes
Servings: 2

Ingredients:

- 2 1/2 cups water
- 1 lime, juiced
- 1/8 salt
- 1/8 tsp dry mango powder
- 1/8 tsp ground cumin
- 1 dash black pepper
- 2 tbsp sugar or sweetener
- Lime slices, for garnish
- Mint leaves, for garnish
- Ice cubes, as needed

How to prepare:

1. Start by throwing all the ingredients into a food processor.
2. Blend well until fully incorporated.
3. Refrigerate for 1 hour then garnish.
4. Serve.

Nutritional Values:

- Calories 105
- Total Fat 1.1 g
- Saturated Fat 0.4 g
- Cholesterol 2 mg
- Sodium 84 mg
- Total Carbs 2.1 g
- Sugar 3.3 g
- Fiber 0.6 g
- Protein 2.4 g

Conclusion

Plant based diet provides a win win solution for everyone looking for a healthy diet. It protects those from saturated animal fats who are suffering from cholesterol and cardic diseases and on the other hand its save people from acidic red meat and other animal produce which cause toxicity, high blood pressure etc. This cookbook provides a holistic view point on the plant based diet compromising of its basics, the known advantages and all the Dos and Donts. Moreover range of plant based recipes are covered to meet everyone's routinely needs including plant based smoothies, breakfasts, lunch, dinner and desserts.Besides these recipes, the book gives a three weak diet plan which enables better adoption with complete ease and convenience especially those who weekly prefer to plan their meals.

Made in the USA
Lexington, KY
04 November 2019

56583394R00092